Sweet Geometry

Sweet Geometry

Poems by

Leslie Contreras Schwartz

Cover design by Shay Culligan
Cover image by Jeffrey Keenan on Unsplash
Author photo by Hagit Bibi

ISBN: 979-8-90146-906-4
Library of Congress Control Number: 2026938749

Kelsay Books
502 South 1040 East, A-119
American Fork, Utah 84003
Kelsaybooks.com

Acknowledgments

Thank you to the following publications, where versions of these poems previously appeared:

Academy of American Poets: "The Bell," "A Body's Universe of Big Bangs"
AGNI: "Long tall fence"
ANMLY: "Illness in Origami," "Echolocation with Self and Body Parts"
Black Earth Institute: "Convalescence, in Flames"
The Cortland Review: "Bone Fold"
Cutthroat: A Journal of the Arts: "Aubade to Missing Mothers"
Guesthouse: A Panoply of Modern Writing: "Nights"
Houston Public Media: "Fever Tree"
Huizache: "Playing God Like Girls," "Dallas, 1983"
Luna Luna Magazine: "Xibalba" (as "Quarantine")
Pleiades Magazine (Periodic Element Folio, edited by Rosebud Ben-Oni): "A Body's Universe of Big Bangs,"
Rogue Agent: "Day 45: Post-Infection Tachycardia," "Night Roost"
Zócalo Public Square: "Palinode to Rescue" (as "Anti-ode to Rescue")

Praise for *Sweet Geometry*

From the sickroom where we all hunker down, Leslie Contreras Schwartz beautifully sings the body electric, a body that suffers and emerges sanctified if not always healed. *Sweet Geometry* is her vivid chronicle of the long journey into illness and out the other side.

In poem after poem, we journey with her through a version of Xibalba, the underworld of death gods from the Mayan creation story. In this underworld, we must confront the basic truth about being human: how vulnerable we/our bodies are. Contreras Schwartz masterfully balances the dream of good health, human arrogance towards the body, and the politics of who gets to survive.

As Bruno Schulz, the Polish writer, once said, "speech is [our] metaphysical organ." Throughout this book, we see how important the intersection of speech and metaphysics are—a lake is described as a 'great cosmic socket' and Valentina Blackhorse, one of the first members of the Navajo Nation to die from COVID-19, is eulogized by the voices of people who loved her.

Illness sharpens Contreras Schwartz's lyric reckoning; this is a poet at the height of her powers. *Sweet Geometry* asks, "Who dares to have a body/in this place." To me, it is clear that Leslie Contreras Schwartz does. It's a daring and political act, to connect sickbeds the world over through these moving, essential poems.

—Connie Voisine, author of *Calle Florista* and *Rare High Meadow of Which I Might Dream*

In *Sweet Geometry,* "[w]e enter through a wound, / we leave in the same wound. With daughters. / With sons." In her compelling latest collection, Leslie Contreras Schwartz opens with "Kaddish," based on the Jewish ritual prayer for the dead, on Higgins Lake where "the moon with its blank palace will wax with its many rooms, / but you cannot use them."

And so the speaker finds other ways, to not only survive but to continue to bear witness and speak out, in this moving, lyrical account on illness, motherhood, hope, and "un-prayers," too, during the COVID-19 pandemic and its aftermath. And when she faces challenge after challenge, often without answers or relief, she too responds in kind, without flinching, without compromise: 'against sky / breaking into American-grade light, // against each other and sister, / my sister, what leftover dawn / are we, of our no mothers?'"

—Rosebud Ben-Oni, author of *If This Is the Age We End Discovery,* finalist for the 2021 National Jewish Book Award in Poetry

Contents

Praise for *Sweet Geometry*

I.

Body of Water 17
Kaddish 21
Kaddish 24
Quarantine 26
Long tall fence 35

II.

Day 45: Post-Infection Tachycardia 41
Nights 43
Night Roost 44
Leper on the Lawn, by the Front Door 47
Illness in Origami 49
Fever-Tree 51

III.

Aubade to Missing Mothers 55
Playing God Like Girls 58
Momma 60
Dallas, 1983 62
Mother and God Box 64
Doll, Mother 66
Creature 68

IV.

3 a.m. at St. Luke's Hospital, April 2020 74

V.

Race/Ethnicity of Houston's 2,050 COVID-19 Deaths as of March 12, 2021 (City of Houston Emergency Operation Center) 79
Tina, Dibé Yázhí 80
Vanielle Blackhorse 82
Tina 83
Tina, Dibé Yázhí 87
Chummy and Dibé Yázhí Play until Sunset in Kayenta, Arizona 89

VI.

Body and Cosmos 93
Palinode to Rescue 94
Convalescence, with Flames 96
Echolocation with Self and Body Parts 98
A Body's Universe of Big Bangs 100
Green, Veins, Room 103
Convalescence: Come 104

Notes 107

Dropping the baby in the grass,
falling on my arm in the parking lot to stares.

Some errant code tangling my roots,
body held back by the hands of black earth,

silt clouding my eyes and thick in my mouth
so I can't say what I want or need.

What my hands won't hold, how my lungs
snap in the heat and sun.

I birthed her and the world drained its body of water
from my body, the liquid I can no longer make

for my eyes, throat, organs, mind.
A name as foreign as my body now: Sjögren's.

To go back, in that turn of the tide, before the swell
and boat bobbing, lilting, to swim in the heady

daze before the sun gets too bright and dizzying.
No blank-eyed stare of the sky set over us.

I cradle the baby in the hospital bed
years before vials on the nightstand, when sharp

virus orange lights our figures aglow,
laced with toddler limbs wrapped through mine

as we twin sleep with our arms thrown up
and our mouths slack.

Watch us beautiful here, mother and child,
watch us mimic each other's breath like shadows

as our bodies do what they want to do.
The water laps at our edges,

lulls at the lips where our bodies
spill over and spread.

The currents lap
and rock our single bed.

Kaddish

Higgins Lake, Michigan

The water on the shore's lip frozen thin.
The frozen parts glisten in a sheen
of sky with no eyes.

Behind me, a cathedral of pines set to expectant
reach, crooked arms set away, still but heavyweight
inside those veins. You don't know which way they'll swing,
if they could, and what doesn't give way,

sometime or tomorrow?
I watch the waves of the lake blue-grey and rolling
in that great cosmic socket. Watch them thrash themselves
at the ice's jagged edge. Five million names,

five million nine-hundred
thirty-five thousand six-hundred
and sixty-eight names and counting.

Bodies that gave up in waves,
and here beat their names
a bloody noise beneath a murky surface.

No smoke filling up the sky, no gash for a single golden eye
set unblinking overhead. Lucky, my two feet on the shore

imagining flimsy hospital gowns and nightclothes
beating into wings. What right do I have imagining a world
where the only bodies in ice are those skating

above it, here, on Higgins Lake, Michigan,
when the lake gives into winter.

Your names sanctified in a winter that lasts as long
as it takes. Blessed be the world where a God is possible

and summer comes when it should. The ice melting
and no chance for a last look behind.

Blessed be the crowd come to rest on the summer's shore.

Where they kick off their socks and shoes,
bare skin and sweat beading.
Delicate wildflowers, slender
and quivering around ankles. Some cloudless sky.

You would eat from each other's hands,
you would hold an apple or a sliver of cheese
to a beloved's mouth.

Here the lake beats high-noon waves
against the rocks, a green pool belonging to the universe
of your two blessed feet.

Lovers' clothes left behind besides dunes
and the sand's wind-dusted wings.

No terrifying queen sounding bells.
The place where I watch the waves and sky wrestle into solid
ice

a fever dream: I stand up, I am running down the canyon
of our street, the sky hissing in sickly rose coils

past the elementary school and the turbulent rivers named
Shivering Canyon and Murmuring Canyon

toward the bayou ten blocks away,
to Brays Bayou bridge next
to the Jewish Community Center,
the mail stop, the grocery store and the Russian general store.

The bayou's banks filling with rain,
Xibalba's flooding sickness,
the bayou ready to break over the edge
of the concrete embarkment.

A hurricane yawns overhead,
its great arms weaving sheets of rain

and I run until my whole
body stings.

Arriving with a familiar feeling,
I'd reached the crossroads of four paths
leading into the heart of Xibalba

where the heroes were undone.

Yesterday, or a millennia ago
when my people

who'd faced death with story,
and plunged

into the world's gouged-out mouth,
pulled from underneath by vines
shimmering in phosphorescent ultramarine, verdant green;

there, next to galvanized steel pipes in the bayou,
black water spitting against the muddy banks,
forcing our families into the attics, the roofs.

There, with feathers of quetzal and cotinga,
winding its long neck around our ankles,
our throats.

With the city,
the bayou festers and
we drown.

I view my family on the bank
from under the water

caught in a wide
terrible jaw.

I'm part of its foul mouth, its teeth
gnashed with bodies and hair,
pus and vomit.
I'm slick between two shattered bones.
Fever, the shaking body—

I look up. Cast in that blue brilliance
that *glimmers through the gaps*

the faces of my children, my husband.

And there it is: the sound, the beating,
the drum.

The Lords of Death at the ballcourt
of the gods pounding the divine rubber ball
into the skulls

of any mortal who dares to play.

Suspending time, the gods pound against the sacred
walls and eviscerate human bodies like twigs,

grind heroes to dust
and throw their white ash into the river.

I wake up wheezing
and choking. I sleep wheezing
and choking.

Xibalba floods our bedroom.
Who dares to have a body
in this place.

My husband wakes me, feeds me soup,
water from a straw.

I suck medicine through a tube
powered by a noisy black machine.
The box sits like a tank between my legs.

It has been weeks since I'd left either the bed,
or the couch. Laying, blinking,
and when awake, staring through the window,
at a wall, at one of the children's faces.

Breath through a tiny tube,
gulped in small pockets.

You're here, the doctor said on the phone.
Be grateful.

The air rations itself
as I sat outside wrapped in a blanket,
feeling shorn.

I can hear the ballcourt and its echoing chamber.

My children play in the front yard
while the light gasps through the leaves
of the oak tree on the yellowing lawn.

Underneath the world—or beside it, along it,
between it—there, the pulsing
of electric cotinga, indigo, gleaming,
glowing its unearthly blue,

its color not of ocean blue,
not a sky flanking the earth.

Day 45: Post-Infection Tachycardia

I'm running and there are flashes
of lit-up sky in split knuckle Vs or is it my eyes
throbbing past the knot in the tree
and my skull that keeps tripping

or dropping down legs in thick

litters   festering clots

and blue-ing baby the baby the rush of blood and tangled hairs
    in fingers
                its grip can't see but I feel all the bones

and thin ledges splintering / out of my hands

to the running the branches the scrape the bottom up

black purpling grip on my
ankles & running

/ and run   there's no set time or end to the burnt horizon
    up
up the birth canal in a hairline turn / and there must

be a choke or a cough in the hard bush but it's silent

to base of the neck / who's timing and /

I'm running so I won't hear it or know it and be it with this
racing and the rubbing of my feet and thighs in the one spot
that is dragging

this loosened bridge swaying / I'm clawing and drinking and
spilling and swallowing /

the decking is cracking /the
piles headfirst tipping / and
breaking and /
flat out now it's coming I'm
coming / get up don't
facedown they're leaving it's
going not going / get up

Nights

The curtains stripped from the rod.
Just the night-things, the window
and self left to deal.
I suspect this is done, alone.

Night Roost

The body talks to herself in dead-of-night, grooms
carefully like a cat, licking the furry and blue-tinged spirit
into agreement:

Tomorrow you will not walk.

You will lose walking and lifting.
You will wake up choking.

The old one, laid out on the bed like a slash in the sweaty
sheets
puts her gaunt face in the hands of the girl:

the one secreted inside with a handful of soft fat
and collagen plump, gardenia-lipped days.

She plucks the old eyes, black
grapes, eats skin then pulp.

You have to fold body parts to get to the purpling
-inside skin, into the slick baby face. Behind her thighs are
feet,
then legs, pickled in formaldehyde.

I love you so
and so, she tells the other,
the elder running
from her lips.

Together they eat their own origami heartbeats.

They passed through this
danger and did not die,
though everything was done to them.

—The Popol Vuh

Seeking the duende, there is neither map nor discipline.
We only know it burns the blood like powdered glass,
that it exhausts, rejects all the sweet geometry we understand.

—Federico García Lorca

I.

Body of Water

The baby broke me
in half—

first, her body quickened
under the taut cotton fabric

of my shirt, foot sharp
against my ribs, a ripple of leg under the skin.

The rush of spilling water
past my ankles to a puddle at my bloated feet.

My muddied canvas shoes,
my shirt soaked and stuck in wrinkles to my thighs—

then I'm bare feet-first in my husband's hand
and sixteen hours of hard climb

where I could not see the room except for the sharp
angles of the black and white clock, its brutal march.

A hospital-edged glare and the sea of blue uniforms crowding
in their face masks as I roll feverishly. Hands swarm,

a thousand bees checking pulse, oxygen levels, IVs,
hovering above face and limbs like antiseptic ghosts.

Somewhere far away, a distant shore of myself, my reddened thighs
with the doctor's latexed hands deep inside my body

as he pulls the baby's head, draws her out with a suction cup—
her crown of black hair blooming.

Was this the moment my body turns and attacks
itself, then never stops?

Her fat flesh and smooth down of lanugo,
black and feathery, staring down at me from a swaddle of pink
and blue,

a ridiculous striped fitted hat. A flash of the divine
donned in water-colored clothing—

how incongruous
as her eyes glistened like a fawn's at daybreak!

The room dims, I stare,
the light leaves the room in swaths.

The steady pull of myself to the undergrowth
of trees, buried with the world unraveling itself:

amid the joys of first smiles, the baby rolling herself
across the floor in sea-green pajamas with a ruffle on her butt,

coupled with the years ahead when my mouth won't form
words,
my legs held down by invisible weights, my hands clumsy or
useless.

all still and perfectly kept—the leaves, the shapes of paths,
breath's flutter—

a future of skaters' coats billowing
above the lake that merges with sky, crystalline.
Their bodies afloat like wings.

A delicious winter to last seasons—

But the room you left won't sing, the walls sit in a single
closed mouth.
Tonight, the moon with its blank palace will wax with its
many rooms,
but you cannot use them.

I dream of God, of holiness, I dream of a world where holiness
lives
where you don't leave and leave the room. No one calls me
lucky.

Kaddish

There were frozen feet, row after row, purple and still. There were cities, towns, stadiums, emptied except for wild animals set out from hiding, a rogue mask or sweater curled around a railing on a bridge, wet and limp from melting snow. There was the labored breath, the difficulty talking, the coughing and the weakness, one person then the next. There were whole beds connecting around the world from one sickbed to another, lit up upon the screen in red. There were the lights pulsing in red circles, patches to represent hundreds, thousands, millions. There was the city, with people on their balconies, screaming or singing, clapping or hysterical under the terrible face of the moon.

There were the closed eyes of the walls, the chairs, everything inside the home turning against its owner as its garments became smaller and tighter around the throat, a belt around the pants, shoes shrinking and clothes becoming like children's clothes, thin-layered, ruffled, infantile, the smell of sour milk. Nothing fit. The room barren. There was walking in circles or up and down the hall, counting, pacing like a panther, and licking the walls, eating all the food to the back of the cupboard. There were the children, their faces pressed against the windows, their saliva dripping like tears as they made gestures at no one passing by. Rainbows in windows to show a sign of life.

There were driveways and front lawns, balconies, or fire escapes wrapped up in imaginary electric wire that no one could cross. There was the incessant glow of the cell phone, the television, the laptop. There were the bodies, on the screen, the bodies in the bed, the bodies being transported by windows, through the streets. There were our own bodies, suddenly urgent, muskier, more present, alive, as if we'd never noticed our own smells, our own heartbeats. There were the sanctified bodies—still there but barely—past coughing and hacking, feverish and clinging to sheets and life with ragged breath, but silent now, in a coma, in their dreams making one last-ditch plea for some type of God to emerge from nonexistence and snake Herself through the respirator, give back breath. There is the other sanctified, the drunk woman on Facebook in a tank top and underwear signing karaoke, the teenage girl posting selfie after selfie, breasts and arms and lips all blending into one image, may these women and their bodies be sanctified, may they be glorified, may their grandmothers and grandfathers sitting in retirement homes without human contact be dignified, may we honor the bodies with remembrance, the mass of people falling into the great cave at the lip of our driveway curbs—our very lawns and sidewalks passageway to the Underworld—blessed, praised, glorified, exalted, extolled, honored, elevated and lauded. Prayer that there is a place imaginable where this one is not imagined, I was never sick, you never saw me in bed for a year, I did not need you to lift me out of bed—

Quarantine

The lights in the bedroom
flicker.

I lay in our bed
listening
as somewhere an animal

is beating its
tired head.

In a half-dream,
I walk to the door
and shout, *Who's doing that?*

And nothing
but this violent drum,
its ancient beating, blow

after blow, drowning
my words.

Thought exhausting, afraid
to sleep but longing for it with the same urgency

for breath without pain, to sit up
without lung-crush and stupor.

To fill my thoughts
with something other than every second
of half-breath.

Was the sound growing nearer?
Was it a foot banging a door, my daughter
running circles in the living room, feet pounding?

Was it the neighbor at some task
again that required loud pounding and screeching?

Questions to latch
onto in my mind. I entertained them.

Whatever beast
wrestles, it marks time
against my skull.

My son whispers but I cannot hear
as the thumping drowns out his voice.

The thought of speaking rolls over my body
with its ten-thousand-ton wheels,

I roll over with eyes
in slits, lucid enough
to see

my five-year-old boy jumping
on the bed, aching
the springs
with his bare feet.

We are alone here

with the Framer
and the Shaper,
the Maya sacred one,

the feathered serpent
curling on the ceiling
with its open jaw—

my son laughs as the God
crackles luminous
rifts through hell's river
on the walls,

clicking its broken teeth together,
straight into my lungs.

The roof flies off, and my boy and I
lay beneath the open womb of the sky.

He crawls near me,
wraps his skinny legs around mine
underneath the coat of blankets,
its tassels of stars.

Momma, I hope you feel better soon.

At the lip of Xibalba, the underworld of death gods,
a shaving of light breaks from the bedroom door.

I see my baby leave and
don't want to close my eyes.

In Xibalba, there are many trials.

I am in the House of Cold.

In the *Popol Vuh,* the sacred Maya text says
these rooms are coated thick with frost.

The wind howls cleanly through the door
and clatters hail against the walls.

Its whistling shrieks the emptiness.

My son is whispering against my hair.
I cannot hear because the cold
blows and snaps.

I sleep, I shed skin, I don't die.

I wake up hacking, shallow breath, I'm falling—
I fall into the Scorpion Rapids,
I fall into the river thick with pus,
I fall into the river seeping blood.
The House of Knives.
The House of Jaguars.
The House of Bats.
The House of Darkness.
I fall into the river full of dead bodies.

One morning or one night, or the next day,
or the night that was yesterday and before, tomorrow,

Only death lapis lazuli of the sacred,
a deep cave at its center with a rattling tail,

in its hue the blood of childbirth,
the whitened lips of the dead,
the infant's violet wail—

I hear its pulse and ring,
long and unraveling,
a cruel silence
with a terrifying bell inside.

I had already heard the bell.
I had already imagined my children without me.

I rest my head back on the chair
and stare at the sky that is no longer the sky.

Now my son's kid sneakers of black and red and white,
flashing lights when he jumps,

my eight-year-old's plastic glittering pink sandals,

both dangling off the edge of a spider swing,
their small hands flayed out and waving,

the laughter, her sigh,
to the canyon
below.

Long tall fence

of the body, its dream-memory of a fleshy hand
and the baby's belief in ownership

of the sky, herself.

An I with a name bright behind it, lit up,
and Mother's checkered shirt,

illuminated refineries decorating the skyline with flickering
earrings,
pinks and reds crossed with yellow stripes, a plaid.

The sight the scent of my own milkiness looking over a
shoulder.

Tucked in with a blow—
lightning and white-out—
a plunge and a wall.

This is mine.

The thought persisting through the body's hit
and the sliding down.

The smoke of the bituminous shale body
burning underground,

centuries long:
the I with a name without limit.

Many days of lying still, of wild belief sewn with long black
hairs,
Mother's shirt, the crosshatch plaid,
her wispy bangs against my chin,
shaking the side of a white-lacquered crib.
Sewn: that the body belongs to anything.

And the mother of my childhood
works inside the woman's body.
Its slice of childhood at work
inside my woman's body.

Feet tied to an imaginary metal chain.
A link to the jeweled refineries, to my mother's necklace

my eyesight blurred by honey, the sweetness
of belief in the American body,
the brown body, the sick body.

The body gives.
Drops the cup. Refuses
the legs their freedom to walk.

You will not,
she said, from inside.

I do not.

It, however, does—even though the world does not believe
in the invisible, the invisible body's invisibility.

Cruel jokes of cough after cough
and months bedridden, mind
locked up in vials of pills, sucking on albuterol.

The heart's chamber the room
Mother made up, tchotchkes

and a recliner, lighter fluid and a wad of newspaper,
industrial waste at her feet.

She sets everything on fire from inside.

It's surprising, every time.

The moment passes, returns, reverses,
worsens—a thing of stupid catastrophes
and back-talk.

I did believe in power over my body—
it hangs in innocent stripes on the flag.

I sang of the body's autonomous beauty,
the mind's leash and collar—

But look, at the pacing of the mind, its trailing along the gate
of the long tall fence

at the city's forgotten limit.

I carry the blow,
which is to carry all our mothers' blows.

Now it's mine, so what?

Let mother out to pasture.

Give yourself up, water shedding from your hands.

Turn and turn to wildflowers in the fence.

II.

Together they edge and crease, googol-fold.

Pressed, creased, made one with a hardline turn:

body the tool, the pattern-maker, reaching inside
this many-inhabited place of herself and herself,
multiplied to a million ones.

Handsome now slipped inside
one another. Neatly folded,
and swallowed whole.

Fully formed, now down they go
through impassable
vines,

using body as rope
into subterrane—

Here they hang
upside down,
bat wings curled
around one
another.

Night dosing, the roost
steams the cave,
their guano a precious
snow flurry.

Mother claw, gripping

and the wrestle against
bone's barbed wire.

I'm the thing rough twisting
of feeble into prism—

I'm holding off the slice
of the spirit,
yes, the vitality—

yes, the watertight
selfhood
resistant to crush.

Leper on the Lawn, by the Front Door

I go outside to dress
in day, its half sun and—

the neighbor does not wave.

A rustle of white-blue sky
trees tossing heads and outright

skipping. Whether I'm here
or not—I checked messages.

How could you
infect other people   *Keep your sick*
Here's a list of all the ways you have wronged me
I'll light a candle for you

I'm here, now, beside me the gulping air and a treble
in the vermillion banana-leaf plant next door
or the pluck of the swing in mid-air

my half breath, and my daughter flying.
The certainty of her dark crown.

Above her the feathered green shook,
then stilled.

Heavy, down to the knotted-black chair.
I'm stilled and shorn. I know my neighbors now.

If there were wounds to bear, I'd leave
a trail of blood crossing the street

just to tell my neighbor Shabbat Shalom
and go fuck yourself.

Wishing for that wound,
I drink a steaming hot sip

of a thousand cups
to a rollercoaster heartbeat.

I don’t quit.

Illness in Origami

Inside ourselves, we
are folded:

lines for future folds, reference
points, hidden or interior lines.

An old recipe of heart songs
and nightmares.

Folds get unfolded: the blood, the veins,
the cells, the bones.

Collapsed, secreted, warped.
A traveling purse that takes a virus whole
and lets it burrow into the spirit-matter.

This is how a year of illness
sheds leaves from a fever-tree.

The in-and-out sight of your last love, his dark lashes.

*

Bloody coughing, half-sleeping, breathing cut
and rough,

do the body and the mind exist in the mirror images,
combined with double squash, swivel fold? Everything hazes
    as
        they

exist side-by-side, in this common valley of sick.
Points are brought together at a single spot of destruction

to believe that we are so irreducibly complex—all it takes is one
blow.

Folds get unfolded, in any case. The inside reverse fold, used to
change
direction of a flap, and inside the body's well sits mountain,
valley, rabbit-ear folds creased along the walls:

birthing flaps that wave like tattered flags
the white flutter of surrender
or the triumph of a woman's skirt in spring.

I'm going to die like this.

*

Winter has ended and still I could not sit up.
Leave me here, I tell my husband.

*

The mind the body the mind the body

I am the object combined in three easy steps:
pre-crease forever, then collapse and collapse.

Fever-Tree

A mouthful, polite, tidy, fed
in pills: circle or square,
blessed and cadaver white

and pale baby blues,
the circus purple,
fluorescent gelled candy.

They hang from a tree,
its boughs dressed for going out—
lights and sparkle, earrings, chain—all that.

I pluck and swallow
under this makeup smeared sky.
The thing assuaged, lest it chew and bite.

My body glistens like a downed branch,
or sharp, a weapon slick with oil.

The fever all night
again, grows
roots and limbs.

Near daybreak, there's the hand tool made of bone and carpal:
dull-edged and exact. I'm choking for air and need the damn
thing.

Suck in, suck in, little roots to the bottom of the lungs,
its tiny pathways. I would use a knife or a chisel to reach
breath,
I'll cleave in two—

The vials are empty.

The giant roots break open.

The hospitals are full.

III.

Aubade to Missing Mothers

Mexico's shadow, this country casts.
Lights its stores' dawn on the afterglow of missing mothers.

Generations of half-blooded mothers. Full
& blooded. Unraveled helix, part indigenous

& part Spanish entanglement. Double helix
colonized and thread barren.

Sick mothers holding
colonies to the tongues.

Mothers burning lightbulbs
for the united states' hospitals, factory warehouses,

mothers without mothers, flat on their backs

pushing and straining through birth
canals without mother's hands.

Their backs for every bead and *at the hour of our death.*

And the doctor's hand all the way
back. In the hallways mothers,

on convent floors and black eyes.
Rolling pins, with cast-iron pan eyes.

Hot irons and leather-encased,
belts with buckle-eyed. Selfie encased, filtered.

Papered doll cut up pasted hanging
on sidelines and off clotheslines and washeteria ghost mothers.

The fevered wet cloth & no mothers.
Menthol & salt, sana sana to the chicken feet
all-night and all-day mothers.

Underbed cuy cuyed and drunken
limbed men draped on child mothers.

Trapped mouth and earthen mothers.

Cellophane mothers
wrapped air-tight
and shipped through Amazon by mothers.

Lost connection
with no bars or airtime, mother. Mailbox full.

O Mother of mothers, for you bats and nightingales
skirt the ceiling and flinch for what you ghost.

And the baby grabs for the crack
underneath the root.

Mother-of-none, see the baby gumming long
hairs from the marrow

of a country of lost tongues and families.
No one tell her there is no nest.

Baby mestiza gums
the air in fat gulps or half and half

for sugar, for breast.

& when she wails
the bats fly out one by
blackened one to hang

to any darkened crack,
to click an ultrasonic pitch.
And the sisters come

out and bounce echoed cries against trees, against sky
breaking into American-grade light,

against each other and sister,
my sister, what leftover dawn

are we, of our no mothers?

Playing God Like Girls

There is a girl with a wagon of ragdolls.

There is a girl with a wagon of ragdolls in front of a bayou.

There is a girl with a wagon of ragdolls in front of a stream of slime-crusted water alight with chemicals called a bayou.

There is a girl with a wagon of ragdolls in front of a stream of slime-crusted water alight with chemicals called a bayou where she and her friends play with grasshoppers and fish in the stream and don't know any difference between goldenrod or dandelions, between fish and tadpoles.

There is girl with a wagon of ragdolls by a broken fence to her family's backyard where a drug dealer chased an addict and she watched from her bedroom window.

There is a girl with a wagon of ragdolls in front of Green's Bayou, it is 1990, and she is done with dolls and is throwing them one by one into the bayou.

In two years, her father will lose his job and they will lose their car and their house. Her mother will throw her clothes onto the front yard and tell her to leave, not only once, because her mother is sad, or depressed, or sick, and there is no 1-800 number, only belts and belt buckles and soap operas.

There is a girl throwing ragdolls into the bayou playing God.

There is a girl throwing ragdolls into the bayou calling an end to childhood because she says so and wants to beat it there.

There is a girl who stood on the bridge over the same bayou years later after being pushed out of her mother's car. There is a girl with a backpack and a fistful of clothes and a book standing on the bridge looking at the bayou, the place where she threw a wagon of ragdolls, and said I'm just getting started.

There is a girl who left the place with ragdolls, the bayou of chemicals, the mother pushing her out of a car, the clothes on the front yard, fists at her head, inside her. There is a girl who believes in God when she loves a girl and they hurt each other because what do they know about love, throwing themselves out of cars and into boy's backseats, cradling their secrets in each other's bodies. There are two girls, with ragdolls for bodies, and how they learn to throw each other into different kinds of open mouths, how they learn to love what hurts and how much they can stand. As God, standing together like this over bayous and men, they choose to be thrown, they choose the wagon, the ragdolls, the boys, the men, each other, and what kind of cruelty they decide to call love.

There is a girl with a wagon of ragdolls, in front of a bayou, in front of a stream of slime-crusted water, where the tadpoles glow phosphorescent, where the grasshoppers sing hymns and the sun sets low and fiery atop the girl's black-haired head, and she burns blue, the ends of her hair carbon and hydrogen, she radiates.

Momma

She had no face, only hands
with pointed red nails.

Any mistake the child made—a spilled glass of milk,
a cry too loud,

existing at the wrong time with her long brown braids—

there was the grab of hair at the scalp and the drag.

Clear as glass, the body travels to meet wall,
the thud of face hitting floor, the body meeting floor

and its blackout dream.

Magic, almost beautiful, as the body levitates
against the worn leather belt.

The mom levitates to memory: a child tied to a bed
and her own mother.

Mother was still the child bought to be a maid, an elderly
    woman's caretaker.
Broken-in animal. It was the 50s for decades in mother's
    mind.

Everything I begged, I begged with daughter, with child, with
broken baby, and a limp hand. Mother. Mother, she cried.
Look what you've done.

She would pull me up to see her, eye to eye, her fist holding
the crown of the head of hair,
the whitened choke that caught in my throat. Clearing down
all the trees.

You do not know what I am capable of you did not know how
long I can hold you like this

and my daughter, in my arms twenty years later, the room levitating to find Mother's bony hands—I look down to the inner parts of my baby's fleshy cheeks. Her blessed fat legs and feet, pinked, rosy and sacred.

Momma she called me. Momma I could not see except the hands at my crown.

Momma, I touch her crown, its nest of black curls.

Momma left in the limp of my left leg,
the pain in the spine. I close my lips.

Her hair will only be brushed like down.

Her head will only be flowered.

Dallas, 1983

Mother shielded my head,
held my face against her left shoulder
hard and bone, the sharp of barely 90 pounds.

The wind belting up leaves, newspapers,
rubbish in seething aerosols besides shops
selling cowboy boots and boutiques
of gossamer children's clothes.

The milky thin spread of Momma's skin.
Beaded necklace in faux lapis lazuli
from the cheap jewelry her birth mother sold
kept in the back of the closet with my blood-tinged milk
 teeth.
The red-nailed sharp finger grasp of mother's hand.

I wanted midday sun and the earth green carpet
of my grandparents' tiny house.

Instead, her palm at the back
of my curly head and through the gaps
of a baby blanket, its pale lemon and rose threads,
I saw the street thrashed and clawed by an unseen body.

The shape of my mother: her black hair sending trees
 crowning
and bowing in long strands.

Presented as the world to my four-year-old mind,
things whipped away with a hand suddenly
swollen, a skipping or a back hand belonging inside me,

a sense in a newly formed cerebellum fissure,
an infantile knowing built upon the peach of grocery-store
    baby food.
Crusted metal spoon and the corners of my mouth, my own
    sugared saliva.

My refusal to eat the putrid dollops, at the rental house on
    Hopper
or the one on Froley. A wet shock against the tongue,
the force of a hand and a spoon.

But this day I laughed with glee, how it rained sideways
on us and soaked my head, pressed us together—
a checkered blouse against a doll-sized white turtleneck,
matching plum skirt made of felt, too expensive and
    precious—

inside the beginning of a storm, what I'd later recognize
in the way it suffocated and stripped the roads in turns, front
    lawns born
naked and bone-tight in an hour, slick as an oil rig—

Mother and God Box

After the scribe's box, 15th century, Granada, Spain
from the Art of Islamic Worlds in the Museum of Fine Arts, Houston

In here you make me strange. A necklace, a sweet, a nun,
hidden
under your door.
I live in this place of your torn light, married to lines and stars
written in your door.

Dear, how we meet each other inside. Wild in the bazaar of
longing, but private, kind.
Lightning in sacred forest, rendered in bright sea-blue. Earth
and
first fruit, we hold tight under
autumn & the door. My fat finger under the door jam.

Plentiful the food inside! Full tables, open doors, your tender
cup!
(I see through the crack).
A garden and storm sing a million skies? It must always
thunder
under the door.

But I'm content to exist in your squares, without the plum or
the
multiplying
inside, even in the mind. The hinge doesn't break and never
closes.
Please, open,
open the door.

The pretend-sea of your eyes cleans me. & I live another day.

If I unlatch the planets stop. No windows, without houses, no
mountain, or sky exist
under our door. No door to your door.

I carry faith, my beauty, in your fat bottom lip. With each
suckle, I
invent the gifts under your
door. & the door. & the box. Besides, inside, above and below.
Tomorrow waits, I, to be born
again under our door.

Doll, Mother

She made of her, with black lace,
a baby widow, dowager

with clod heavy shoes
inside the chest.

The plaited hair she threaded.

Her fingers
pulled strands
with a fingernail.

Dissecting the head
in the exact lines,
braids run with white
scalp, the interlace tight

as the labia. Locked and holy
against the skull.

Pet on the shelf.
Her little hair shirt.

A girl gets what she gets
when she opens her legs.

How the daughter waited
to pull out the eyes,
unravel the stitched black orbs.

Loosen the heart
of its spine,
seam rip
the feet, the legs,

each single strand
of black hair. Open the legs.

A ruined doll,
who cannot walk or run
or speak.
Held up
broken in the air.

Much better
than mother's
plaything. Better
than mother's anything.

Legs splayed and letting out.

Creature

From under the earth, in a root that cracked open. This creature was born, furred, and twisted in vines. Umbilical cords tied around its neck, into no mother's arms, an underworld changeling. I was there—how it mewed, barely, set its clawed foot into the earth and heaved to the surface. What was it? This being that pushed itself out of a bountiful, rotten place, a sort of human bud, wolf-like, weak and pale—as if it could grow into fierceness but not yet, half deep-sea fish with blighted eyes and translucent skin, part rattling tail, small, tight-ball of a predator with an unseeable poison weeping from its eyes. I watched as it wheezed there, in the curling grass, and remembered how it felt to be sick with pneumonia at three years old, my grandmother visiting me in what I thought was a cerulean gown, like the Virgin Mary, but with red lipstick and eyeliner that made her wide eyes wider. My biological grandmother, Ninfa, who wore a gold chained necklace, smelled like Mary Kay rouge and powder. She gave me a tiny notepad from the paper-mill where she worked and told me to pray to my angels. I do not remember being taken to the hospital after her visit.

The creature is a girl, breathing from gills, sputtering on land. The creature opens its mouth and out spills dirt and vines, creepers, the blackened roots of goldenrod, tadpoles, swamp slime, nats and hibiscus blooms. I move closer. She stirs, moves to sit up: this thing spit from the earth from the mating place of snakes and scorpions, seeps blood and pus, hair twisted into nests. She has my face, my mother's, my mother's mother's and hers. I fall into the cavern of her eyes. This is how the fever began.

I press my face to you, Mother. Hold my cheek to your carmine robes, sweaty and unladylike, desperate, my legs wide open, my skirt hitched up. You smell rotten, sickly, but I hold on, and I prepare to labor for you. No longer newborn, you are gargantuan, you are ancient, you are a skyscraper, you are a civilization buried in sand. I press my hand to the layers of your gown. I cannot see you. I'm not able to see you. Hush, you say. Hush. Sleep. I dream of the kind of life that lets me sit outside with my children today, while you drag me to the center of the forest.

IV.

Office visit February 28, 2020
Dr. XXXX XXXX MD
Reason for Visit
Asthma
Fatigue

Visit Diagnoses
Upper respiratory tract infection
unspecified type - Primary

Office visit March 9, 2020 Dr. XXXX XX
Reason for Visit
Cough
Shortness of breath
Chest congestion
Chest wall pain
Body aches

Visit Diagnoses
Exposure to COVID-19 virus – Prim
Exacerbation of asthma, unspecified
severity, unspecified whether persiste
Viral syndrome

Administered medications
Depo-Medrol Intramuscular

March 12, 2020 Results Letter Dr.
XXXXX XXXXXX Chest X-ray Normal

Telemedicine visit April 14, 2020 Dr. LXX B
Visit Diagnosis
Exposure to SARS-Primary
Cough
Moderate persistent asthma, unspecified whet
complicated

Medications
Fluticasone-Salmeterol (Advair/HFA) 230-21
Inhale 2 puffs into the lungs
MCG/ACT inhalation
2 times daily
Aerosol

Levalbuterol HCl 1.25
USE 1 VIAL (1.25 MG) BY
MG/3ML Inhalation Nebu
NEBULIZER EVERY 8 HOURS

AFTER VISIT SUMMARY
XXXXXX MRN: XXXXXXXX DoB:XX/XX/XXX
3/21/2020 4:37 AM Baylor St. Luke's Medical Center
Emergency Department

Instructions
Call your doctor Monday

Read the attached directions
Shortness of breath Adult Easy-to-Read (English)

Today's Visit
You were seen by JXXXX XXXX SXXXX. MD

Reason for Visit
Chest Pain
Shortness of breath

Diagnosis
Shortness of breath

Imaging Tests
ECG 12 lead
ECG/EKG Interpretation
XR chest 2 views

Your End of Visit Vitals
Blood Pressure 145/92
Pulse 102
Respiration 18
Oxygen Saturation 98%

ED ECG Interpretation 3/21/2020 3:22 AM Rate is tachycardic. Axis is normal. Clinical Impression: non-specific ECGECG reviewed and does not meet STEMI

Office visit March 16, 2020 Main Campus Testing
Reason for Visit
COVID-19 Suspect

March 16, 2020 Status: Final result (Collected 3/16/2020)
Results: SARS-COV-2, NAA Not detected
COVID-19 test was negative

Your test for COVID-19 infection is negative. While it is very likely that you do not have a COVID-19 infection, it is possible that you could have a COVID-19 infection that was not detected by this test. For this reason, it is important that you monitor your symptoms. The following list contains the symptoms that suggest possible COVID-19 infection:

- Fever
- Cough
- Difficulty breathing or feeling short of breath or out of breath
- Loss of your sense of smell.
- Loss of your sense of taste.
- Sore throat
- Muscle aches
- Chills or shaking
- Headache
- Runny nose
- Nausea or vomiting
- Diarrhea
- Fatigue
- Confusion
- Chest pain or a feeling of pressure in your chest

Office visit May 21, 2020 Dr. LXX BXX-XXX
Visit Diagnoses
Chest pain, atypical
Tachycardia
MCP (mitral valve prolapse)

Telemedicine Office visit October 22, 2020 Dr. XXXX XX
Visit Diagnoses
Suspected COVID-19 virus infection – Primary
Close exposure to COVID-19 virus
Moderate persistent asthma with acute exacerbation

Telemedicine 1/20/2021
Diagnosis
COVID-19
Weight loss
Asthma
Inflammatory Arthritis
Sjogren's

Result Date: 03/21/2021
Name:
SARS CoV 2 AB (IgG)
Value: **Positive**
This test is intended for use as an aid in identifying inviduals with an adaptive immune response to SARS-CoV-2, indicating recent or prior infection. Results are for the detection of SARS-CoV-2 antibodies. IgG antibodies to SARS-CoV-2 are generally detectable in blood several days after initial infection, although the duration of time antibodies are present post-infection is not well characterized. At this time, it is unknown for how long antibodies persist following infection and if the presence of antibodies confers protective

3 a.m. at St. Luke's Hospital, April 2020

The waiting room is empty, except for three homeless men and me, and another man with blondish hair who's dressed in a light blue button-up, sitting patiently like a phantom. An ER doctor and a security guard stand around the homeless men and shout, plead, then threaten until they get up and leave. The sliding door hisses as they exit. In the middle of one of the largest medical centers in the world, in a city of more than seven million people, the hospital waiting room is devoid of people, save two.

The lights jolt and fade, the man falls from view. *Where are my children?*

The nurse asks if I am safe. Squeeze, pulse, heartbeat, sanitize, slow and raggedy breath. Her eyes glisten above her mask, ribbons tied at the back of her head like a schoolgirl. Then she falls away with the man, an away place where the homeless men have gone, down the hall through more sliding doors. A doctor appears above me, the IV clinking when he swarms in, his brown hair wild. I can see the veins in his hands while he speaks. They are shaking.

He sighs and twists his hands together like a woman in a Victorian novel before she faints. There are no beds, he says. There are none. I look around for the smelling salts. He coughs and chokes, and spits out a black body, a bee. In his hand, it moves hideously in mucus then flies above his head.

He's trying to say something that is neither reassuring nor informative. Something maudlin like a lover in a Victorian novel? If he did, it would make perfect sense. I'm closing my eyes into slits to see if it helps clear up the situation. He coughs another bee, two at a time, then four, then a hive. His mouth widens the more he tries to speak, and he sputters out bees until the throng of them have fled his body. The hive occupies the private room. My heart beats to a machine, a twinned din. I'll be right back, he says. I'm relieved to be left with the bees. I'm too tired to explain myself and they seem to know something instinctively, some secret sachet stashed inside my body.

The bees land on my body, one by one, above the thin sheet, which I pull up to my chin and watch them wander without judgment. My shoes and clothes sit clothed in plastic by the door. I'm worried how I'll leave, but not as much as I should be. Right now, I am weighed down by an entire black hive—I can think about it later.

My eyes open and I'm in a cold room, the metal bedrails sputtering. My hands are above my head. I am without sheet or gown. *Where are the bees?* They have fled, it is too cold. A machine whirs and rattles, and simpers then stops. I'm covered with a sheet that was bunched at my knees and a set of new hands push me down the hall, through a maze of empty halls, passing doctors and nurses in masks who are going in haste but making an effort to appear slow. The hands fall, the doctors and nurses fall, a woman in uniform without a mask who is cleaning the floor appears briefly and then falls. I'm waiting for the doctor. The monitor screeches, and the bees flood into the room again. This time they do not explore. They go straight inside me. What a relief, they must have found the source. The bees black out the overhead light as they rush in, having found some nectar, intoxicating must it be, at the back of my throat, in the soft lining of my lungs. I am content with the surety of Mother Nature.

The doctor has fled. There are no footsteps in the hall. The bees are ripping up the IV, worrying the tape over the insertion. A few make it past the needle and pull it out. My blood splatters white against the walls. My blood curtains the floor. The black bodies form a gauze over the wound. I'm starting to rattle. I must leave this place.

I grab my belongings and start the slow walk to the ER exit, stepping on bees that fall from inside my pants to my feet. *Where is my family?* The streets are emptied, streetlights glowing for no one. I taste sweetness, fear's precious flower. The bees and I feed on its marrow in the night quiet. Then I open my mouth to the sky, and they fly out in a dark trail.

V.

Race/Ethnicity of Houston's 2,050 COVID-19 Deaths as of March 12, 2021 (City of Houston Emergency Operation Center)

Black (427) 21.94%
Hispanic (1,107) 54.02%
White (393) 18.94%
Asian (116) 5.70%
Native Hawaiian/Pacific Islander: (1) 0.05%
Arab: (1) 0.05%
Native American: (1): 0.05%
Unknown (4) 0.20%

Nationwide adjusted excess all-cause mortality was 6.8 per 10,000 for Black individuals, 4.3 for Hispanic individuals, 2.7 for Asian individuals, and 1.5 for White individuals.

Navajo Nation COVID statistics, March 4, 2021

Ethnicity	*Population*	*Cases*	*Cases per 1000*	*Deaths*	*Cases per 1,000*
Navajo	*173,667*	*29,794*	*17.2%*	*1,187*	*6.83*

Residents of the Navajo Nation have been 4 more times likely to die after contracting COVID than the average American, with 172 positive cases per 1,000 and 7 deaths per 1,000.

Tina, Dibé Yázhí

Valentina Blackhorse, September 2, 1991–April 23, 2020

Valentina Blackhorse did not survive after she contracted COVID-19.

Valentina Blackhorse was one of the first Navajo Nation residents to die from the COVID-19 pandemic, whose community was disproportionately affected by deaths from the virus. She was a 28-year-old pageant winner with a one-year-old daughter when she died.

Yes, she was my dibé yázhí, little sheep.

We had a luncheon when she was little, a traditional event. I said Sit still, don't run around. There she goes, climbing on top of everything. She's a funny person.

She loved the flowers that bring the hummingbirds. Roses. The bright ones.

My baby, she helped us a lot. She helped her Dad fix the vehicle, learned how to do mechanics. That's how she was.

Since she was a little girl, she wanted to know our traditions. She learned how to dance to go to the Pow Wow. At 7 years old she was talking about being a Pow Wow dancer, little helper.

She had a lot of plans, even when she was small. To be a Navajo Nation president, or a council delegate. She talked to students with the elders, to tell the young to talk Navajo. I thought she was going to make it.

Vanielle Blackhorse

We used to drive two to three miles out of town. Park. Sing. Dance. Laugh.

We danced in the car, driving and laughing. She loved metal and rock, the band I Prevail, and the smell of rain. In Kayenta it hardly rains. Oh, and dancing to WWE wrestling superstar entrance songs! Oh gosh it was the best doing silly things with her.

She came over every day after work calling out Chummy!, when she came in. She never greeted us by birth names. Chummy, the name my family gave me. My family still addresses me with it. I called her Tina.

I miss Valentina shouting my nickname when she would come over.

As teens we'd sit or lay on her bed all day, every day. Talking and cracking jokes. I'd listen as she wrote and read poetry, or what she called "raps." We laughed so hard later about it. She was brave and never backed down from what was in front of her.

When we got older and moved out of our parents' house, had daughters, we'd still go to her old room and lay down on the bed, but this time with our daughters.

Tina

When we were younger—I was really young—we were playing war and I put a Navajo basket on my head, pretending it was a hat. We both got in trouble because in our tradition we're not supposed to put the basket on our head or we would stay short.

Ha! I'm the youngest but I'm also the tallest! Valentina was shorter than me but taller than our oldest sister. She loved taking photographs of other people but not being in them. She said she'd take a picture of my little family when she got better.

She hated to clean or cook. Said she'd get a maid or chef when she was older. Ha! That never happened.

She was going back to school, now that Poet had turned one. She said she'd have a small dinner for Dad's birthday that month, for her boyfriend's birthday. She and her small family.

I had a five-month-old girl and my oldest turned one, Poet's little twin. Like us. Everyone called us twins, and we were always together as children. Poet looks just like her. We grew up in a small town. So people knew who our parents were and they would come up and ask us Are your parents so and so, and they would mistake Valentina and I for twins. We would always be seen together, we were never alone, always with one another when growing up.

We were going to dance with our girls in the Pow Wow arena.

She loved dancing, even though her knees would become swollen, even though it gave her so much pain with the rheumatoid. But she kept going because she loved dancing.

I still needed her here. She knew things about me that no one else will ever know. She literally took all my secrets with [her] and I will do the same. Gosh, she was my best friend and the best sister to me.

Back in seventh grade she went on a school trip to New York for about a week. I was so sad and lonely that we cried when they left on the bus.

I don't have a bond like I did with her with anyone else, almost like a twin connection and a few days after she passed, I lost it. Every time I felt down or I was in pain or something was wrong, or vice versa, we would know something was off with each other, and we would call or text to check on one another. That's how close we were. We just knew each other so well.

Our plan was to start dancing again with our daughters. As of now, it's hard to step back into the Pow Wow arena without her by my side.

She wanted her daughter to know our Navajo traditions, to speak Diné. She encouraged young people to learn Navajo.

She organized writing contests to encourage young people to learn Diné. I helped her buy giveaways and prizes, to read the essays. She organized back-to-school supply giveaways.

But she focused on our Navajo language, how much it meant for the younger generation to learn and keep the language going.

She loved all holidays and gave everyone presents, little gifts, everyone. Buy V-grams from the sellers on the side of the road—those baskets with chocolates, candies, balloons and teddy bears—and give them to all of us on Valentine's.

We called her little sheep because our mother said she wouldn't keep still as a baby, like a little lamb. That's how she was.

She loved winning pageants, although she'd apply at the last minute. Miss Western Navajo. Miss Monuments Valley High School. Miss Diné College. She believed in our tradition. We used our herbs and prayed so long before they took her.

I remember seeing her on a pageant stage for the first time. She looked like she belonged up there. She was very shy growing up but once she got on stage and in front of the judges, she wasn't shy whatsoever. It came naturally to her.

I cannot go in the arena without her to dance. She wanted to, but I don't know that I can.

We were worried because she'd been coughing. At the beginning of COVID last year, the jail here didn't provide proper PPE, not until it got really bad. Robby didn't get proper PPE at the jail as a correctional officer, not until it got really bad, and exposed us. She took care of him til he got better. She was an administrative assistant for the Navajo Nation, and started working from home. They both got COVID in the beginning of it all here on Navajo Nation. Most of the Navajo Nation didn't provide proper PPE to the jails unfortunately until it got bad.

Her first test was negative. When Mom and I talked to her, she was struggling to breath when she spoke—

I could feel something was wrong the night she passed. I couldn't explain the feeling—it was a heavy feeling. I remember I just started praying as hard as I could and I started crying, then 20 minutes later my mom got the call. We prayed so much. Then she passed. Like that. A flash.

Tina, Dibé Yázhí

She always smile. Say hi mom and hi dad. Wave her hands when she came to the door. I say Why you always do that, wave like that? To everyone, she did that. She was funny like that. She talks funny, jokes, nicknames. She and Vanielle were always joking, laughing.

It is not the same. They were very close.

I wish my baby was still here to help us. Empty chair. Every day she came to our house, to clean. Help with a lot of things. I thought she was going to make it. But she didn't.

April 23, 2020, the day after her positive test, at 10:30 we got the call that she died. I said, Let me see my baby. I went to the clinic. Walked into the room and pulled the cover off her head, pulled off the mask. She was still hooked up to the tube in her mouth. I just held her hand. She was just laying there, sleeping. That's what she looked like, like she was sleeping. I held her hand, talking to her.

I go to Farmington to visit her grave. Her headstone is a valentine. I tell her, Baby, I love you. I miss you. I will never forget you. She was my baby. I made her a memory garden for the hummingbirds.

My daughter points to her picture and I say that's your awesome auntie and I tell stories.

People come up to me in town and say "You look so much like your late sister." It hurts so much. Everyone said we looked like each other, like our daughters look like each other.

She came over to our house every day and every weekend, all day long. She helped clean our house, helped us with everything. What does this letter say? I'd ask her. And she'd tell me if it was important, or Don't worry about it. She'd treat us to meals and when we'd ask her how much it was, she'd say Don't worry about it, shimá. You don't need to know.

Chummy and Dibé Yázhí Play until Sunset in Kayenta, Arizona

Mom keeps an eye on the girls through the window.

In the front yard, inside the fence, their own world

set into the sand and scrub between their sunburnt legs, knee to
knee.

This is our store. This is our school. Here are the people.

Dramas requiring toy guns, romance with Barbies, wrestling moves

needing practice like the headlock or the walls of Jericho.

Tina was good at those moves, throwing a football pretty far too.

Little Diné girls' shadow huddled in the sand against mesa and sky.

This is our store. This is our town. This is our home. This is our
family.

This is my sister, and inside her my mind thinks her thoughts, dreams her dreams.

When one goes, so the other, their laughter twinning through
the
small town.

You're a Blackhorse girl, no? Neither minded being mistaken
for
the other.

Laughter with heads drawn together. Their bodies thrown to
the
ground with how funny

the world was, how wonderfully joyous when a sister

loves you and you never ask why. The same way the night sky
binds itself to the Earth:

I love you, I love you from here, near or a long way off, I love
you
sister of mine.

There is nothing truer than two girls sunburnt and sweaty

made from the same thing, sharing the same blessed earth at
the
same given time.

On that yard they played and made plans, the dog watchful on
guard.

There is no other Vanielle. There is no other Valentina.

VI.

Body and Cosmos

March 2020

Left to the sick-chamber
the odor of the sick-sweet weeds
floating. Night comes.

Inside the bedroom,
seascape hushes.

Around my bed,
mouths open and grow
from the still, briny water.

An underwater cosmos,

my body knows
it can make uncelebrated planets,

how I'd triangle the sky with my ashes

make geometry of my dust
into barely visible stars.

My son is crying at the door
and I cannot go to him.

Palinode to Rescue

Inside us runs a map of our cells un-mapping
in small gulps, a finite road with no rescuers.

I'm waving from that dead-end where the weeds
wild and lower their necks. The treefrogs gulp

and call up night, relief that doesn't come.
The only respite is inside the cell, its fixed membrane

that unfixes and warps, the nuclear envelop that contracts.
Mitochondria tethers or isolates, withers or livens.

Messages sent or not.
The powerhouse, its electric grid

pulses beyond sight and away from bodies.
We are not dotted in that countryside

this side of the galaxy.
Stars' light currents and passes us.

We are located in its trace
away from the power electric, its house

and spinning. We are not the prime movers,
only shifts, an eye half-closing. The un-mapping inside

mirrors the un-mapping rolling out, an animal scroll
let out and flattened. Where are you taking me?—

my daughter says. It won't hurt, I say.
Only sting a little.

We enter through a wound,
we leave in the same wound. With daughters.

With sons. I put my mouth to it.
It will not stop letting out.

Close your eyes, I tell her. The sun drowns
at the end of the road. There is no waving.

There is no leaning, no levee. I hold her up.
I pretend this is rescue.

Convalescence, with Flames

I light no candles and entertain no thoughts.
My bed loves me and sheds me down as I turn

& turn with a sweaty face, the velvet underworld
pulling me with its roots. Wrists wrapped in bead of rosary.

I light no candles for you, fool with your rolled-up eyes,
coins over your sockets. I twist and cough and sigh,

my un-prayer, un-lighting. No one with light
may enter this room. No one with candles and springs,

pulsing with daylight and flames, confetti and caked-on
    makeup,
wrinkling their eyelids in jest.

I want mascara brimmed lakes racoon-ing the face. The shut-
    up
        shiver
and knees that break and fumble through pitch, half-busted.

I light no candles and want none lit on my behalf.

It's the shedding that beds me
and turns me down.

The bed's sweat the honest friend, shedding
niceties with rank down. Un-prayer,

torn from twisted and fallow
tongues.

A cough born from godfeet,
the last dregs of her wine.

What the present feeds, mud seep and fester.
It speaks of presence. It speaks of here.

Echolocation with Self and Body Parts

It's the eyes slit into walls, half-open lids
that tricks. The lips beneath the eyes blue & frost-bitten.
Corpse pose. But a crowbar jams against cut and quartered,

clicking tongues to find the jigsaw of other parts.
A foot in the door, a silent wrenching turning beneath the
ground.
Nearing exhaustion, slit eyes with lids half closing. Half
breathing.

Feeling for the one other body part, a hand, a rib, a foot,
a labia at a time. *Where are you*, the inner thigh calls to vastus
lateralis.
Furrows of corpse flower, quartered and twinned yet firm
against cuts & crowbar.

A jaw's gotten free and is having dinner with the dandelions.
Behind the supper party, a knee and a femur knock on the door
with cracked walls, shutters half open. *Let us back in.*

Outside loose limbs make a cacophony with their reaching
and clacking, hitting elbows into table corners, crowns into leg
bones.
Knocked out into corpse pose. Waiting vultures in fours
opening beaks like crowbars.

The unpeopled people make slits into walls, can see half
dissolving selves in parts, whole, or half-rendered.
The crowbar useless to the coffin.

But it's corpse that feeds the fauna, forests the tree its crowns
& only the mouth drops into the earth, only voice textured in fur,
velvet in fissure and sediment. It can never be lost without its tether.

From under the earth, waiting to hear what I'm doing
just yet and what mercy opens its eye.

A Body's Universe of Big Bangs

A body must remind itself
to keep living, continually,
throughout the day.

Even at night while sleeping,
proteins, either messenger, builder,
or destroyer, keep busy

transforming itself or other substances.
Scientists call these reactions
—to change their innate structure,
dictated by DNA—cellular frustration,

a cotton-cloud nomenclature for crusade,
combat, warfare, aid, unification,
scaffold, or sustain.

Even while the body sleeps, a jaw slackened
into an open dream, inside is the drama
of the body's own substances meeting

one another, stealing elements,
being changed elementally,
altered by a new story

called chemical reaction.
A building and demolishment,
creating or undoing,

the body can find movement,
functioning organs, resists illness—

or doesn't. Look inside every living being

and find this narrative of resistance,
the live feed of being resisted.
The infant clasping her fist

or the 98-year-old releasing
hers. This is how it should be,
we think, a long story carried out

to a soft conclusion. In reality,
little deaths hover and nibble,
little births opening mouths
and bodies the site of stories.

The tales given to us, and retold,
never altered, and the ones forgotten,
unremembered or changed,

until this place is made of only
ourselves. Our own small dictators,
peacemakers, architects, artists.

A derelict cottage,
a monumental church
struck in gold, an artist's studio

layered with paints and cut paper,
knives and large canvas—

the site the only place
containing our best holy song:

I will live. I will live. I will keep living.

Green, Veins, Room

Glow from the backyard,
the spreading oak spreading.

A breath toward the leaf-flame,
a child's plump cheek and bare
feet. The children are fighting,

pulling legs and long arms. Green in the room,
green setting to bruise.

A slice of sky and a room.
My loves at home and the flown
open curtains.

Sips of air perfect and palming,
my loves inside the room
of my chest, it's flimsy walls and hallways.

I'll take it, just like,
push its course
through my long veins.

In the river or the puddle,
the hot heavy air,

I'll take it and hold it, tight grip to air.

Convalescence: Come

Tonight had just been tonight, and now round it comes,
in tonight's jacket and yesterday's same shoes.

A little ache where my toe touches the tip,
one for every day I've walked and back
again in my mind.

Tonight bruises, the needles they tracked for names,

the body flutters and slips,
walking in today's shoes.

Slipping on the edge of a terrible song
and the sky pregnant
with sunset and beautiful gray soot.

Through the notches of blinds,
the image sinks into lap,
a cup of crushed pigment of the world outside,

its shimmering ballgown and elegant wrists.

The dangling diamond earrings the woman makes of her feet
jogging outside, it melts everything in her wake.

Somebody loved me enough
for stillness to arrive.

I plea to want nothing.

I walk to the edge of the street curb.

I walk to counter creases, to sinks and seat backs.

Let me want nothing else.
I walk to wanting nothing else.
Something glittering, turning
My children into kaleidoscope fractals

Red sun
Grass indigo
Their dark hair

Notes

In *The Popol Vuh,* the epic poem and sacred text of the indigenous Maya people, Xibalba is the underworld where twin heroes challenge the gods of death, facing brutal physical trials. The twins defeat the false deities on the ritual ballcourt. After defying death, the twin heroes become the sun and the moon and herald the creation of the first peoples—the Maya ancestors—who were made flesh from corn.

Quote in epigraph: *Popol Vuh*: *The Popol Vuh: A New English Version,* Translated from the K'iche', Michael Bazzett (Milkweed Editions, 2018).

Poems on origami include lines from: *Elementary Differential Equations with Applications,* Third Edition, C.H. Edwards and David E. Penney (Prentice-Hall, 1994); *Origami Design Secrets: Mathematical Methods for an Ancient Art,* Second Edition, Robert J. Lange (CRC Press LLC, 2011).

"Bone Fold": a bone folder—a tool used for centuries, to bend paper into an exact fold—is traditionally made out of bone, wood, or plastic.

Body Chart includes doctor's notes, results, and portions of medical paperwork from 2020–2021, personal to the author.

Poems about Valentina Blackhorse and her family include transcriptions from first-person interviews with sister Vanielle Blackhorse and mother Laverne Blackhorse, conducted February through March 2021. In addition to interviews, details about Valentina Blackhorse's life and death were gathered from news sources, especially "Valentina Blackhorse, Navajo Pageant Winner with Dreams, Dies at 28," *New York Times,* Simon Romero.

"COVID-19 Data, By Race/Ethnicity" includes data from the following sources: the City of Houston Emergency Operations Center; "Racial Disparities in Excess All-Cause Mortality During the Early COVID-19 Pandemic Varied Substantially Across States," *Health Affairs,* Volume 40, No. 2, Maria Polyakova et al.; statistics used from the Navajo Nation website (accessed March 4, 2021); and "Navajo Nation Surpasses New York State for the Highest COVID-19 Infection Rate in the U.S.," *CNN*, Hollie Silverman, Konstantin Toropin, Sara Sidner and Leslie Perrot, May 18, 2020.

About the Author

Leslie Contreras Schwartz is a multi-genre writer, a 2021 Academy of American Poets Laureate Fellow, the 2019–2021 Houston Poet Laureate, and the author of the 2022 C&R Press Nonfiction Prize winner *From the Womb of Sky and Earth,* a lyrical memoir. Her five collections of poetry include: *Black Dove/Paloma Negra* (FlowerSong Press, 2020), a finalist for the 2021 Best Book of Poetry from the Texas Institute of Letters; and *Nightbloom & Cenote* (St. Julian Press, 2018), a semi-finalist for the 2017 Tupelo Press Dorset Prize, judged by Ilya Kaminsky.

Her work appears in *The Paris Review*, *AGNI, EPOCH, The Missouri Review, The Iowa Review, [PANK], Verse Daily, Pleiades*, *Gulf Coast*, and *Houston Noir* (Akashic Books), and *The Best Small Fiction* anthology, among others. Recent work is featured with the Academy of American Poets' Poem-a-Day series. She has collaborated on or been commissioned for poetic projects with the City of Houston, the Houston Grand Opera, and The Moody Center of the Arts at Rice University. She is a graduate of the Warren Wilson College MFA Program for Writers.

Contreras Schwartz is a poetry and nonfiction faculty member at Alma College's low-residency MFA program in creative writing and has taught creative nonfiction and poetry workshops at Rice University and Stanford Continuing Studies. Contreras Schwartz is a Jewish writer born in Houston, Texas, with Mexican American and Mexican roots that extend back several generations in Houston and Texas.

www.ingramcontent.com/pod-product-compliance
Lightning Source LLC
LaVergne TN
LVHW090615110826
845146LV00001B/400

* 9 7 9 8 9 0 1 4 6 9 0 6 4 *